Walking
into
Daylight

poems by

Basia Miller

Finishing Line Press
Georgetown, Kentucky

Walking
into
Daylight

Publisher: Leah Huete de Maines
Editor: Christen Kincaid
Cover Art: *Sagittaire*, linocut by Pierre Cayol
Author Photo: Jane Shoenfeld
Cover Design: Laura Star

Order online: www.finishinglinepress.com
　　　　　　also available on amazon.com

Author inquiries and mail orders:
Finishing Line Press
P. O. Box 1626
Georgetown, Kentucky 40324
U. S. A.

Table of Contents

I.

What Draws Me to the Other Side 1
Turning to Sunshine 2
INSCRIPT: *The Immediate Life XVI* (Paul Éluard) 3
A Used Tire Prays to the Perfect Circle 4
Why Do I Run Away? 5
Happy Hour 6
Cowardly Honeysuckle 7
Dovecote 8
Gardener with a Different Compass 9
After Noah 11

II.

INSCRIPT: *I Live like a Buried Treasure* (Pierre Seghers) 15
Ministers of Roofing 16
Nothing New Here 17
On Painting Trees with Pastels 18
The Sculpture that Feeds Me 19
Bridges and Birdhouses 20
Backyard Tree with View of the Sangre de Cristos 21
Night of Forgetfulness 22

III.

INSCRIPT: *I'm Just Emerging from Darkness* (Pierre Seghers) 25
Aspens and Remains of Wildfire 26
Navajo Mountain, Utah 27
A Granite Arrow Speaks 28
Two Still Lifes: Deer, Hen 29
How Grandma and I Did the Wash 30
Yucca Street Overpass 31
Incident Outside Truckee 32
The Medicine Man Chants the Mountains 34
INSCRIPT: *When I Die, God, What Will You Do?*
   (Rainer Maria Rilke) 35

IV.

INSCRIPT: *Atlantics* (Francine Caron) 39
Umbrella Unhoused and Looking for a Home 41
Magician in the Weeds 42
I Feel My Prayers 43
St. Brigid in a World of Change 44
Prism of Life 45
In the Garden of Guan Yin 46
Coeur gourmand 47
Grand'mère Térésine 49
Walking into Daylight 50
Montségur 51

To the memory of my grandmothers

Caroline Cain Durkee and Sarah Elizabeth Hastings Miller

I'm just emerging from darkness.
I've known the underside of things
at the edge of awakening.
          —Pierre Seghers

I

What Draws Me to the Other Side

My eyes stare back at me from a puddle
after I've run into the rain,

after I've let my fingers run along the narrow
paragraphs of a *New Yorker* story of the violent death

of a young mother. We two women,
one on the page rippling my imagination,

and the other, me—my empty eyes reflecting
up from the water.

We stack loss on loss—her body stilled,
and my failure to feel a bond between us

in spite of having touched the words.
My heart continues, *thump, thump.*

A chill seeps across my neck and shoulders.
I reject the scene, twist away from our faces.

I want to flee the water's surface and
the memory of print bleeding on the page,

the city concrete where she lay.
But no. I'll make myself steady

and keep walking by this stream.
The image will linger and awaken my heart,

so that I am able to grieve her death.
The least I can do, the first necessary thing,

is to bring one woman back to life.

Turning to Sunshine

On this bright day, the workman Hugo stuccoes the wall
around my new windows. A ten-inch aluminum square

he calls a hawk lies on his forearm. There's a handgrip
underneath. I can't help but imagine a hawk alive

and Hugo a falconer. The generator revs to mix more stucco,
the noise rising and falling like a baby's cry.

I was to be my parents' sunshine, but they had a rule—
She gets her bottle every four hours. My stomach churned.

Hunger hurled its protests from the far end
of a Berkeley railroad flat to the front room.

At the co-op, they traded handmade paper bowls
and homespun shirts for food. Daddy sang,

California is a garden of Eden.
A paradise to live in or see.

But believe it or not, you won't find it so hot
If you ain't got the do-re-mi.

Hugo tips five pounds of stucco onto the hawk. A baby-sized round.
As the generator roars, I relive my parents' submersion

in a chaos of crying, Eden not on the horizon.
I reach for the hawk and murmur,

Hullaballoo is a part of building.
Sunshine aplenty will warm my home.

Give me the hawk, Hugo. Let me mother the noisy child!
I'll mold her gently. I'll give her a chance to be.

While I repair the past, the buzz saw cuts cedar laths.
Hugo lays wet stucco around the windows.

INSCRIPT
The Immediate Life XVI

It's clear out. I put on my hat
As if to exit from the day

Anger under the ugly sign
Of jealousy   the most astute
Injustice

Make this dark sky withdraw
Break its windows
Feed them to the stones

This false dark sky
Corrupt and ponderous

—Translation of *La Vie immédiate XVI*, by Paul Éluard

A Used Tire Prays to the Perfect Circle

O Perfect Circle,
I don't know whether you exist or not
but something has blessed me.

Young, I was a slave to Master Subaru,
going where he wanted to go, turning when he wanted
to turn and, on command, taking him back home.

One fall, south of Eagle Nest, my Master and I stalled in deep snow.
A shovel's clumsy attempt to free us punctured my tread.
It seemed I would rot in a pile of tires near the Rio Grande.

Thinking over my past, I saw
that I was a wheel of misfortune, driven toward disasters,
and I grieved. Then I found a new path.

Now I soar to midstream from safe banks—
blue sky above, minnows and crayfish below.
No longer needing an engine outside of myself,

I obey the laws of nature and the pendulum.
I share this freedom with a girl in pinafore and pigtails.
Even flying through the air we are at home.

Do you live out here, too, O Perfect Circle, or are you
inside me, opening my way? You know from my song,
I'm part perforated rubber tire and part perfection.

Why Do I Run Away?

Why do I run away?
I narrow the space given me
for talking to You.
Your voice echoes and You are far away.

I fill up my time so that I have none left
for attending to my conscience.
I turn away when You call.

I can always find a task at hand.
The quarter of an hour it requires
is a quarter of an hour
when I do not need to be aware
of You watching me

I find myself working with words.
It is not lost on me that
this keeps me from honoring
Your gift to me of insight.

Happy Hour

We're sitting across from each other in the hotel lounge and I think,
It'll be easy at least in this first conversation to exchange pleasantries.

Did you enjoy the Missouri poets? Did you skid on ice last Tuesday?
But the words take on a life of their own, somehow importing

dis-ease into a friendly conversation. Not just dis-ease
but a narrowing patience, the way I imagine it happens

when miners, after years of panning, find only fools' gold. Our
words bully us like piled sediment. My pretty evocation

of an old tire swing evolves in spite of me into a spin
that makes my country days outshine his city nights.

His reminiscence of his dad's success in Vegas,
meant I think as a talisman of grace and humility,

metamorphoses into a song-and-dance
poised on the wine-glass to prove something.

Maybe it's the embers in the fireplace
or the late sun scattered on the tablecloth.

Treacherous undercurrents
twist our golden stories.

Cowardly Honeysuckle

Forest, underbrush, a deer darts through the clearing.
At home I groom an overgrown honeysuckle.
Once I thought it would climb but it's the kind
that mounds like bathtub suds.
It's shown no hint of interest
in the tree-trunk posts of my patio.
It's piled its life upon itself, suppressing pioneers.

My gloved fingers find concealed in the low labyrinth
a coil of tangled wire and three clothespins—
I realize this is its green plan of escape.
There's also a red twist-tie here
from last year's staked azalea.
Which, as a matter of fact, died pointing to heaven.

Dovecote

You on your side of the bed
listen to country-western,
I on mine read Herodotus.
It's going to be a long night.
We lay out ritual words:
Did you lock...? Is the dog...?
An ice cube skitters to the bottom of the glass,
sheepskin slipper drops to the floor.
Will o'the wisp dances outside the door.
Each rights itself alone.

Drawn by the darkness
a flock of doves flies in through the window.
Between us, settling, they mound and shuffle,
align their feathers,
tuck heads under wings,
purr contentment.
Something shifts just a little—
I find your arm behind my head
hand cupping my shoulder,
my head nestling on your chest.
Peace settles in.

Gardener with a Different Compass

I tell him I'd like to plant a rose at the corner
beside the snow-ball bush. He looks at me quizzically
and says he needs to find his compass.

Maybe I raise my eyebrow at the seeming non sequitur,
but at any rate, he continues rather charmingly
by saying that he doesn't know where he is.
He checks his red Toyota truck but doesn't find his compass.

I don't even own a compass.

Trying to be a good substitute, I waggle my hand
at the mountains and stretch out my arms to demonstrate
that my street is kitty-wise
to the north-south-east-west compass points.

He spins awkwardly.
I recognize he is trying to orient his body
to a space larger than the yard.

I ask myself if his wide gestures and general unselfconsciousness
threaten me. I wonder casually if he is high
or if his psyche is just distant from mine.
For that matter, his body shape is unfamiliar, too.
He is tall and wide-hipped with long slender bones
that fold down easily to pull weeds. His thin, stained T-shirt
stretches across his chest. He wears a long black ponytail.
His bandana slips repeatedly from
his large aquiline nose and generous mouth.

I imagine him as a courtier in the time of Machiavelli
or on stage at the Globe.

My psyche spins around, busily trying to assign he a place.
In the past he has spoken of studying horticulture
to become a better worker. He manages his physical actions
by articulating his thoughts as he goes.

I ask him to kill a stump that, though supposedly dead,
sends up shoots every spring.
He says, *I'll take a half-hour for lunch and bring the drill back*
with me. That won't be on the clock. Later, *I'll take an hour for lunch,*
12 to 1, and bring my drill back with me.
As it turns out, he announces at the end of the day that he's worked
four-and-a-quarter hours, with 45 minutes for lunch.

I wish he were not quite so precise. Today, Sunday,
I see that he pulled up from between the stones
a clump of chocolate flowers that brought me pleasure daily.
I should have identified them as defenseless volunteers
since they didn't speak loudly enough for him to hear.

After Noah

I am the ark on high water
carrying a wealth I can't put down.
I'm no longer a tree rooted in soil,
I'm moving along, moving along.
I do not know my native land.

I am the dove flying away
carrying my body through the air.
My wings hold steady and do not tire
but my eyes are weak.
Where is my place to land?

I am the waves alongside the boat
the wind alongside the bird.
I'm moving along, moving along.
All my weight is turned to the search
everlasting and unplanned.

II

INSCRIPT
I Live like a Buried Treasure

I live like a buried treasure burning for self-knowledge
I'm a torch deep inside carried uselessly, that dazzles
I'm clear and baffled; and who was talking about an amalgam,
A desperate alchemy, ruts in scuffled gravel?

I'm a fragile bag of skin, a jigsaw of miracles—
Time-keepers, counters ready to stop suddenly
A mechanism of fluids and inexhaustible springs
soon to flow toward other unslaked thirsts. It's all

unknown: where can one live life with detours like a wayfaring pilgrim
sometimes blinded by headlights? Each suffers his own. They'll pass.
Their fiery eyes piercing the darkness, perhaps they'll perceive me,
isolate me and, without meaning to, rescue me from this stall.

Suppose the Universe were just one man and that man a wee scrap
tossed from dune to wave and back again, dying and surviving
centuries of moments, thrown there by mercy or chance, an irony,
a thin film on the material world, ephemeral, corroding all?

Mirrors are my enemies. Life's an inverted image at the edge
of the Nothing that is Everything. I'm a flux that comes and goes.
The ash of an energy, a drop of foam bursting
millenium after millenium. I try to speak us. That's all.

—Translation of *Je vis comme un trésor caché,* by Pierre Seghers

Ministers of Roofing

Dawn just breaking, vehicles converge on my street,
the plates say Chihuahua, Sonora, Santa Fe.

The crew gathers. Dark pants, black kneepads. Gray hoodies are pulled up,
caps brim-backwards. The guys toss coffee cups and close the phones.

Boots rise in front of my kitchen window, mounting the red extension-ladder
rung by rung, and like balloons, disappear on high.

I hear orders barked between men whose faces I can no longer see.
Shovels overhead batter at the gravel, as if beating out a fire.

I'm at my desk when part of the ceiling caves in and clouds cross the hole.
Debris and Spanish curses filter through the gap and settle on the mantelpiece.

How little thought I've given to the roof! It's been a gaping absence
in my count of blessings, this layer that marks my rooms off from sky.

Now the upended wheelbarrow drops the old roof bit by bit into the dumpster.
Now the crew dresses the deck in fresh tarpaper out to the parapets.

The drama's at its height. Foreman Ruben and red-gloved Marco, handlers
of the fire-dragon, put blowtorch to bitumen, then stomp it while it's hot.

They generate an asphalt spell to keep sun and snow
away from me, my fireplace and all I treasure.

The odor of tar pervades the space. I love the ritual,
and I begin to love the roof that covers me.

Nothing New Here

This afternoon I drove down Old Santa Fe Trail
to the boot repair shop with a plan to perfect
my old walking shoes with new shoestrings. My life
runs a gamut, like matryoshka, from large to small.

Mr. Jacobs unspools a length of black cord—
Do you want 40 inches? and razor-cuts it. His pliers
pinch copper aglets on the ends of each string.

Rows of wooden lasts sway on the wall.
Doll-sized leather boots crowd a display case.
The cash register's perfectly good, he tells me.
It dates to the Twenties and it came with the place.

He goes on, *The city archaeologist brought me a ledger
of Spanish maps of the Tenorio grant.* He waves at the Trail.
Outside was just a path. My family was here.

He shrugs. *Last century's Spanish flu, it's not so long ago.
Take my father's birth and his father's, soon you're back
to seventeen-sixty-five when they built this adobe.
They're nothing new either, animal diseases leaping to humans.*

I say brilliantly, *This one came from pangolins.* Suddenly
he's gone, to return with a dusty album. My curiosity's piqued.
Pangolins look exactly like anteaters—here, you can see.

Ron Jacobs flips to a shot of a pair of tall boots
he built years ago from anteater skin, here in the shop
on Old Santa Fe Trail where I buy my shoestrings.

On Painting Trees with Pastels

My plein-air teacher said, *Put your cliffs and trees in motion,*
make them sway or bulge. She said, *Think about words.*
A writer's vowels bulk up sometimes or fall in folds.

I tried to elide my trees for her, but each stood alone
like a parade of many coffins strewn along a slope.
Still my hand and eye are guided, *What's inside can be displayed.*

Today, rain-cleaned air escorts my early morning stroll.
The centers of hollyhocks, black to passers-by,
share their crimson with one who pauses for a moment.

Today, the roadside aster's buds unfold to be seen.
The neighbors' mimosa hails me with blooms.
My catalpa, leaning sideways, guards my home.

The lesson learned, my life appears in pastel trees.
What's more, clear skies unfurl my energies,
blossoms assume sharp profiles as I swing along.

The Sculpture that Feeds Me

The glazed sandhill crane on my desk
signed DONA ROSA Oaxaca Mexico
takes shape around an ebony S—
from planted foot to jutted crest.
Her beak tilts up to test the wind.

Was it the same breeze
that etched leaves black on a lilac bush
against an ocean of brilliant blue
for a child crouched under the branches
who knew it was an illusion?
There is no story.
Just the enchantment of leaves losing color
and sky become waves.

The sandhill crane remains intact
in spite of her varied travels,
clay companions
and narrow shelves for display.

The long neck, head cocked to the left,
balances the body, wings at rest.
The sculpture rewards close study
but today she's not my kin.

Nothing she does steadies me—
my thoughts tangled in the weather,
cruising half-a-dozen scrambled plans.
My stomach sinks as I read my work,
repetitive and bland.

I return to the crane with tilted beak.
She checks for fish and safe cover; her head
a peaceful swirl in the still cattails and pond.

Bridges and Birdhouses

On a basalt lava cliff,
on a trail silenced and softened
by recent rain,

I pass berry-bushes, vines and grasses
thriving in
the persistent drizzle.

I'm drawn to the timeless space
of dew-dappled ferns
and green moss-covered trees.

As I pass behind drooping fronds
I'm ready to cede myself
and become a part of it.

Suddenly appears a posted metal sign
Wildlife & Riparian Habitat
that shakes me from my trance.

So I'm not here alone. The shrubs and trees,
the satin-gray igneous rock, the violent
angles of descent—all have their guardians.

Clear-eyed now, I see other signs
of gentle landscape-shaping : long planks
traverse a rivulet to join two weedy slopes.

Wrens, chickadees, juncos and tiny tits
circle out from underbrush like Ferris wheels
to finally reach their feeders.

To my gratitude for this amazing place.
I add my special admiration
of all who tend its bridges and birdhouses.

Backyard Tree with View of the Sangre de Cristos

She's a poor example of an apple tree. For a start
her trunk's split in three. She's all arms, no body,
lopsided and, like old growth, wind-bent.
I say her splaying limbs stand for a divided heart.

I imagine myself lakeside, in summer, fingering down
through muddy water to capture a submerged ring,
while she sends fingers sideways, going forth
toward a dream of balance, I suppose, at true North.

This year's covered her in blooms, the same
as if there'd never be another spring. Yet she speaks,
in the way of apple trees, of what's unattained:
her white branches yearn for snowy peaks.

Night of Forgetfulness

For a moment this morning, I lift off the pattern
where I blame the other or myself
for the souring of a deep friendship
or for the way dreams fail to materialize
and, despite the rules and without chalking up the inconsistency
to sloppy broadcasting, I drench with water the slow spot
where the buffalo grass seeds are not sprouting
instead of chastising myself for casting too few seeds,
which, though disappointing, suggests a lack of quality
in the work touted as completed three weeks ago and
ready to be judged on evidence, whereas
this fresh watering translates optimism enough—
something can be salvaged—to parry my instinct
to bury myself again in self-judgment
or bow to the possibility (or likelihood) that the seeds
have been deprived, an idea that came to me
the morning after a night of forgetfulness a week ago
that guaranteed the patch was adequately nourished.
When I was a child on land with a windmill,
unless there was forgetfulness the question of
whether I could bathe in more than two inches of water
would be resolved by reading the reservoir dipstick—
thus does trauma appear down the generations and
between life forms, in which relief for the one translates
into relief for the other. My being forgetful of,
or casting off, the oppressive lid
that bears down on and buries energy,
that tramples and tangles the dream of green grass
(so much that it is a miracle to bypass
the scarcity that haunts me like second nature and allows
this twice-a-day seed-watering to loosen a valve,
as it were) lets me also refill the birdbath daily
with three inches of rippling water
and take a rare chance on planting wildflower seeds
and two bushes of potentilla.
This morning a yellow finch, talisman of freedom and generosity,
balances on the birdbath and makes me feel new.

III

INSCRIPT
I'm Just Emerging from Darkness

I'm just emerging from darkness. I've known the underside of things
at the edge of awakening. I've met myself on the water
in the stew kettles of giants. A pathway of phosphorescence
tempted me to go who knows where. I approached the volcano's eye.
A pilgrim scaling Mount Fuji, I crossed slopes flowing with lava
that had barely begun to cool. Scalded, I gasped in the mad wind
that pushed me and at other times threw me full-length down on the ground.
I had to become other, leave, and wrench myself out of the muck.
It was at sunrise that I lived, with every day greeting a dawn
that directed me toward the West across the remote Pamir range
where, archer, I fled from myself. In the sky I placed my arrows
and shot the royal white eagle. Then I ran down
to the sea that was fringed with foam. Of the white foam I was the salt,
scattered by a different wind over another, gentler land.
I was the wrapping of the whip that would shred the flesh of small birds.
Into my blood's tributaries, I mixed the blood of my women
with other strange tunes and roses, I slit open other poppies.
I built so many palaces and ordered so many domes trimmed
that my cities of limpid air slowly turned into my tombstones.

—Translation of *J'émerge à peine de l'obscur,* by Pierre Seghers

Aspens and Remains of Wildfire

Doubt blurs my plan to visit Jemez Springs—
the road's a bore to drive, the village far,
the foliage likely brown.

Then at the Rio Grande,
when I am close enough to hear it sing,
fiery silhouettes of leaves burn in the sky.

Redondo Overlook: look down
at two black crows, souls surviving, soaring,
round a tendril of asphalt even further down.

Hairpin curves and guard-rails mark the crossing
of Highways 4 and 501. The road flies up
beside the forest, left desolate by wildfire.

Death shines among stones.
Strong aspens cast shadows on my route.
A narrow canyon runs along my left.

These armor me to meet
the ruined Jemez range. The scene, coming unbidden,
looses my tear ducts in a blinding jet.

My courage has betrayed me—
the mountain stretches out ahead, naked
but for white grass scattered over scoured bodies

I gape as the full sun pours over the slopes,
then remember that green shoots, late as it is,
are in the offing—and will make them young again.

Navajo Mountain, Utah

It was over before it began
but my body remembers.
We are friends getting together
after long absence.
We talk about the Peabody mine
and their aunt's dementia.

the next-door neighbor describes
the new Filippino doctor
who comes up to you, lays his arm beside yours,
and says with delight, *Look, our skin's the same color!*

We walk to the valley,
the black dog Randy cavorting around us,
scrappy in spite of his game leg.

Green pines and dusty road
open onto a valley
where gardens and a hogan
nestle near a stream.
Swaths of sunlight fall across a cliff face.

I follow the landscapes receding
mesa after mesa
at the hour
when shadows sculpt stone. It is silent.

The desert hangs outside of time,
existing for itself, filling the horizon
Silver clouds drift in the blue sky.
I float as they do, an atom in the immensity.

A Granite Arrow Speaks

There's a quiet place not far from here
where a long profile of tree-topped hills
has the features of a sacred site.

Just when my car tops the rise southbound
near La Bajada, and the engine calms,
the stretched-out Sandia mountain appears—
notched arrow buried lengthwise in the ground.

The view wakes up my heart, my eyes, my ears.
Even shaded by low white clouds,
the arrow says, *Defend the land.*

It calls us to provide for our first needs:
protecting water rights and families.
It's always there, a touchstone,
when we need to rise in dignity.

An ancient thing, Old Nature, carved
her message in this granite form—
the great earth, like a parent, shapes us.

The arrow of the mountain
speaks directly to our bones.

Two Still Lifes: Deer, Hen

After a painting by Tony Da

Above a line that crosses the painting
at mid-point, an arrow flies.
Its eye finds the deer. Its turquoise barb
carves the *avanyu*'s jaw,
pierces its organs.
From the left, a stick-figure
moves forward, arm
still holding the diminutive bow.
A hunter sleeps in the lower half
below the line that divides and joins
and lets him absorb the dream.

I recall a corner of our yard
where a flashing blade
catches the hen's neck
held between two bent nails
in a chunk of cottonwood.
My grandma drops the axe,
while the remnant flaps
in mad arcs before collapsing.
I etch the scene in memory,
peeking out
from behind her black skirts.

Crackling skin of roasted chicken
is Sunday ritual. For the dreamer
the buck is always killed but never dies.

How Grandma and I Did the Wash

My grandmother, Sarah Elizabeth Miller, was born in 1879 in Sylvan Grove, Kansas. She died in 1977 in Wilson, fourteen miles away.

On washday Grandma sent me to fetch a bar of lye soap
from the cellar. Earlier in the week, she'd poured hot lye-water and lard
into a dented pan, and after it set up, cut it with a knife.

I felt a little nervous, seeing those corners never square,
those cubes never perfect. I worried that it might be illegal.
But it pleased me to run my fingers over surfaces the smoky color
of squash blossoms and smooth like pulled taffy on wax paper.

Grandma stored the bars on dry blue planks in the cold cellar
under the hill where she kept potatoes through the winter
and Ball jars of green beans and the dangerous but perfectly-formed
black batteries that the wind-charger somehow filled.

Outdoors on washdays, the huge cast-iron kettle,
round-bottomed like a cauldron, swung slightly on its brackets
above a wood fire that Grandma started early—
after she'd pumped buckets of water
at the windmill to fill the kettle just as the sun rose.

Nothing distracted us from getting the wash done—
a comfy feeling for a kid like me, always at the center of
unpredictable storms with my parents.

When the water steamed, Grandma stirred the clothes with a broomstick,
a faded blue bandana tied over her hair. The witch with her wand
and the fire with its smoke matched the song in my heart.
I'd circle the kettle, banging it with my own stick to make it clang.

Except that on windy days, to keep the smoke out of my eyes,
I didn't go all the way round but stopped and turned back, over and over,
making with my feet a magic half-circle that would keep me safe.
That's how Grandma and I did the wash in the old days, in the time of dragons.

Yucca Street Overpass

Mornings, my habit is to go as far
as the cottonwoods, then retrace my steps.
But today I circled round,
crossed the arroyo on the overpass.
Cars flashed by, a truck marked PNM, a load of alfalfa.
Beside the walkway, in the weeds,
lay a rabbit—a youngster—its scrawny body
carefully laid out on a white paper napkin.
Across the arroyo I rejoined the trail and went home
over rock-filled gabion and desolate rock-filled plateau.

I wonder, was there a rustle in the grass
then, say, barking and rambunctious chase?
Someone didn't look away or hurry on, but stayed
waiting for her companion to return.
She rummaged through fanny-pack or pocket
for something to spread as a shroud.
She found the napkin, leftover from a coffee shop,
and cradled the wild form
in the fabric of human ceremony.

Incident Outside Truckee

*

It's 4 p.m. near white-drifted Truckee.
Since two our train's been stopped and
no one's explained. Passengers peer
at close-ups but can't tell rabbit tracks
from patchy melt. The conductor's voice
at last. *Medical help to car 640.*
Under the snow there's living and dying.
The Zephyr, paused, faces east.
An unsteady breeze, our Mariah.

*

A couple in the lounge car says,
a man in despair got on at Sacramento.
The train has blocked a rural road—
pickups in line back to the curve.
I hear a shirt-sleeved passenger reciting,
Whose woods these are I think I know...
Under the snow there's living and dying.
Through the window I study drifts
pocked and stained by coal.

*

Safe passage on a train is an article of faith,
routine as ski trails that descend, converge—
yet to the right, a set of tracks
where someone floundered near the T-bars.
The train glides a few feet, freeing the drivers.
Under the snow there's living and dying.
In spite of our wait the announcement of death
(we could have guessed)
brings shock-waves to the others in our car.

*

The death connects chance travelers.
I had a friend who entered a trance…
My grandmother still solved cryptograms …
We lace stories together, sharing memories
to tame unframed space.
Under the snow, there's living and dying.
After the train whistles, we hear on the P.A.,
Next stop, Reno. The cars slide
into motion then gather speed.

The Medicine Man Chants the Mountains

The visitor taps her grandson's shoulder.
Calm down, son, we'll be going soon.
The quavering voice drones on and on.

I distinguish six beats, sometimes seven, then a pause.
I make out nothing more, but part of me is following.
The medicine man sees the four directions rise and come to him.
He names the mountains that guard the traveler's route.

Here in the red sandstone house, the lights are on.
We've finished squash soup and beef stew.
The boy wants to go home.
His great-grandfather's songs don't mesmerize him.

I follow the song that recites the mountains.
The singer wears a Zuni horse fetish whose simple black cord
falls on a blue Navajo shirt. He's ninety-four. All his life
he's helped others find their way home.

Now I'm carried back over his years—he is on horseback,
here near Lake Powell, riding into the wind,
framed by his sacred mountains.

INSCRIPT
When I Die, God, What Will You Do?

When I die, God, what will You do?
I, Your jug, will be broken in two
I, Your mug, will contain a curdled brew
I am Your clothes and Your currency.
Your meaning will vanish with my life.

When I die there'll be no home
where words can offer You a welcome.
I am the velvet slipper that comes undone
and falls from Your tired feet.
Your cloak will no longer cover You.

In vain You'll seek me in that place
where Your gentle glance on my face
found gratitude, but when my self's erased
it will lie down at sunset
in the lap of cold foreign rocks.

What will You do then, God? I am afraid.

> —Translation of *Was Wirst Du Tun, Gott,*
> *Wenn Ich Sterbe?* by Rainer Maria Rilke

IV

INSCRIPT
Atlantics

Upon the baroque Ocean
the androgynous barrier
that we reach from the low land
from encampments of brambles and umbels
from scarified ditches
MEDUSA
with Eyes of furious emerald ARISES
trance and measure of our fragile—human—eye
She who collides with lichens and scoops out quarries

Keltic Fingal of granite   Organ
Songstress of basalt   of amber
She ventures her blackened bliss
her crushed strength
in the drawing of rocky jaws
of yellow-green and moldy tenons
of rotting beams   planted in living sand

Nightlong wonder with her haunting salt
the greenish panic she begets
mother of pitch
and mother of hope by turns
thief of pebbles and metres
expelling clumps of sopping straw
mechanically   like bundles of ashes

Copy of death she boils
she remains silent   she contracts
ceaselessly birthing   arousing
BRIDE trailing trains of crafty lace
growling through rough waves and grave assaults
greenest of greens
possessed   in love with a single shout
a single livid snake   Suddenly escaping

Swelling of the flesh
o crisis   pregnancy
ample theatre   unrolling carpets
of star-studded womb   large with rage
sorceress Sea
fictitious life and real face
striking forges with the Wind

WHEN WILL THY GODS be born ?
When thy sons ?   stars   monsters   Pegasus
OR thy linen daughters ? ... Songs ... Poem

—Translation of *Atlantiques*, by Francine Caron

Umbrella Unhoused and Looking for a Home

After a photograph by Warren Keating

From my balcony I spy a hexagon of blue—
Mam'zelle Umbrella streaks down the avenue
Along with Monsieur Bright Jacket/Brown Shoe.

Where do you fly, Blue Umbrella?
Does hunger make you devour the space
Between our street and distant arcades?
Yes! You crave more of what's like you—
Montmartre's carousel leaves curved traces…
Your straight lines mirror the Pyramid's faces…
Scale Eiffel Tower shapes that repeat your gores!
Spin like the wheels in bicycle stores!
Don't copy Magritte's men in suits
Who hold umbrellas like parachutes
Pasted onto the sky.
You, Blue Umbrella, must fly!

No, wait! Someone's pointing at you—
Ceci n'est pas un parapluie! It's not an umbrella!
It's just a canvas pressed to the wall.
But O, Paris parasol, if you'd rather save
Monsieur Bright Jacket/Brown Shoe from snowfall,
Don't be distressed,
We too are pressed to the wall.
But we create space with dreams of grace!
So fly, Blue Umbrella, fly!

Magician in the Weeds

Clearly, they've said, "Wait here—we'll be along."
She shifts from one foot to the other
this child of ten. But when?

The corner's dry late-summer weeds
beyond my window   hold no promises
could not fund a dream

Her fingernail slices a dandelion stem
she bends it round
sends it through   then loops a second
into a chain of minutes

Milkweed pods split by thumb reveal
black seeds   with lightest keels

three breaths release a shower
of arcs   graffiti
of short duration

the infinite shapeless wait
No one better than she
fills without effort

the expanding universe of time
A whistle across taut green blade
brings the van

swerving to the curb   she grabs her things
door slams   engine revs
wings of silver thistle
shine in the grass

I Feel My Prayers

For Kaia

Most often I give divinity a sidelong glance,
I resist acknowledging the unknown.
I hope everything goes okay, I say
or close an email with a cliche, *May you be well.*
These pass for common currency but hide a plea.
They're like old books with ancient flowers pressed
between the pages.

My body is better at entreaty than my words are.
My nerves tense up when my granddaughter begins to
cross the mountain stream. My muscles mimic hers
as her bare foot reaches for a flat rock, far but not too far.
While she's in-between, off-kilter, a wish wells up in me
to offer her a rail, *May she be safe.*
I steady her with my eyes, then tears roll down one by one
stinging my eyelashes and cheeks.
May these seeds of prayer
support her in the instant and still be there
when she catches her balance again.

St. Brigid in a World of Change

Your smile lingers at borders.
Something on the doorsill
gives you the pleasure of what is not still,
and you pause.

Metamorphosis names the moment
your body unwittingly grasps that
the day is not what it was before.
It's shifting.

We know the signs of early spring—
the wind from the south,
the grass peeking green through snow,
the branch turning toward an earlier sun.

Of course it is not like that for you.
Signals come to you from dimmer, deeper places.
But you smile with the certainty
that what has dissolved will be whole again.

The hot iron bar cools in the shape of a horseshoe.
The broken bone will heal.
With your hand on your heart you feel
the pulse of spring in your veins.

Prism of Light

For Malala Yousafzai

Wherever it's found
light throws open windows
unlatches gates
loosens links that bind our bodies
and tie us to the ground.

Light breaks through silence, Malala,
as you speak to the leaders
of readings for girls
of lessons shining.

Light converted the crack
of black bullets, Malala,
fired point-blank at your temple
where you rode unarmed
in a schoolbus in Swat—

bright images of you
bandaged in Birmingham
flashed on screens and
burst on the world like a prism.

The sight of your courage
inspires us, Malala.
We stand tall
because of many like you,
light-bearing girl.

In the Garden of Guan Yin

I found myself at a loss
and came in need of compassion
You laid a hand on my head
and offered comfort
I caught water from your tall vase
as much as I could take
You led me into the sunlight
and made me whole with golden thread

I bared my head to this warm sun
It has tanned my skin
You laid a hand on my head
and offered comfort
I have seen myself in your eyes
and come more clear
You led me into the sunlight
and made me whole with golden thread

In this land of plenty
where a thousand hands are ready
You laid a hand on my head
and offered comfort
I have spent a while here
beside your door of wisdom
You led me into the sunlight
and made me whole with golden thread

Cœur gourmand

In memory of Marylou Butler

About memories, I've learned
they are not binary—here or gone.

Like landscapes,
some lie in front of you.

Some you need to turn around
in order to see—

or, better yet, like pebbles.
You swish your hand to uncover them

at the bottom of a deep pond.
For example, I've kept this round, purple sticker

from the village of Auvers,
the village where Vincent Van Gogh died.

The trademark is *Cœur gourmand*—greedy heart.
The sticker's all that's left

of a small goat cheese with figs.
The saleswoman in the open-air market

smiled and said,
Eat it right away. It won't travel.

I sat on a bench in an Auvers park
and paired the cheese with bits of a long baguette.

But what I want to talk about is my friend.
She has died, but my heart yearns for *before*.

Every time I came to her door,
her welcoming smile let me know

I was the one she was waiting for, just then.
Today, wisps of green begin to change the landscape.

My evergreens need tending. They call me.
But I delay. *Not yet.*

My greedy heart wants to dwell a while
in the rich shadow of darkness.

I want to stop time in order to see the past
through a different lens.

Just as I save the small round purple sticker
I write to savor memories.

The world has a steadiness and things have a destiny.
This escaped me before.

Grand'mère Térésine

Marie's protected by mud-shoes,
straw hat and leather gloves
against freshwater splash
and rosebud thorns and sun.

At the close of World War One,
her grandmother, Térésine,
daughter of Provence
age seventeen, dug potatoes
in this garden in the Gard,
filled her wheelbarrow
and walked five days upland
on silent roads—no gasoline—
with food for cousins
in the dry Ardèche.

Strawberries, asparagus
and onions still poke up
among the flowers.
Old olive trees and fig trees
cast erratic shadows
on fieldstone walls.

Golden honeysuckle, white marguerites,
yellow syringea are in bloom,
while Marie re-stakes the stalks of iris
just toppled by the six-day mistral.

Walking into Daylight

After a photograph by Siddho

Starting just before dawn, the woman moves slowly,
white scarf with braided fringe over her hair.

Near the black lake a wolf's piercing cry
makes her footsteps tremble. Frost bites the air.

Knives throw bouquets of shadows on canyon walls.
She subdues her heart with a murmured prayer.

Not only wildlife here—rabbits, scorpions, snakes!—
but invisible Ones who've etched signs in cinder and ash.
She walks among ghosts without knowing her goal.

However far she goes will be the right distance.

Now in saffron hills, footprints mark a clear trail.
Clouds delight with their fugitive figures of ancestors.
She follows the sun's path in the sky.

Silver horizons make her aware
of the aging of her body and limbs.
Can one's footsteps be both delicate and firm?

It's easier going now that warmth penetrates clothing.
Gratefully she inhales dry air and,
making the most of her strength, strides forward.

However far she goes will be the right distance.

Montségur

In 1244, Montségur, a Cathar stronghold in the Pyrenées, was besieged. Hundreds of Cathars, called heretics at the time, refused to renounce their faith and were massacred on March 16.

As you approach
the mountain,
dusky blue curtains
disclose layers,
transparent near the
soil, where
striations are distinct—
like fingers etching
brown lines in limestone
or trunks of olive trees.
As you raise your eyes,
the clouds seem
more dense,
masking
mountain contours,
concealing, revealing,
as the
tramontana
blows fierce majesty
or calms to a berceuse.
You imagine the settlement
when the crisis came,
where, behind fortress walls,
women gently covered
children's hair with scarves,
and men sought no options.
Here at the end of the world
you would simply
stay and die.
All life is written
in these clouds.

ACKNOWLEDGEMENTS

Grateful acknowledgment is made to the editors of the following publications where these poems, some of which have been subsequently revised, originally appeared:

Giving Voice to Image 5 (VIVO Contemporary Art, 2017): "Umbrella Unhoused and Looking for a Home"

Lummox: "Atlantics" (translation of a poem by Francine Caron) (2018); "I Live like a Buried Treasure" (translation of a poem by Pierre Seghers) and "Ministers of Roofing" (2019); "Bridges and Birdhouses" and "I Feel My Prayers" (2020)

Malala: Poems for Malala Yousafzai (FutureCycle Press): "Prism of Life"

Minimum Wager: "After Noah" (January, 2020)

Santa Fe Literary Review: "Two Still Lifes: Deer, Hen" (2016); "Backyard Tree with View of the Sangre de Cristos" (2017)

Santa Fe New Mexican: "A Used Tire Prays to the Perfect Circle" (poetry first prize, Pasatiempo Writing Contest 2018); "Nothing New Here" (poetry first prize, Pasatiempo Writing Contest 2020)

Santa Fe Reporter: "Ministers of Roofing" (third-place winner, Spring Poetry Search 2019)

Trickster (Northern New Mexico College, Espanola): "Dovecote" (2016); "A Granite Arrow Speaks" and "Walking into Daylight" (2018)

Voyage Grand-Tournesol (Editions Z4, 2020): "Aspens and Remains of Wildfire" and "Navajo Mountain, Utah"

Permission has been granted to publish the translation of the poem, *Atlantiques*, by Francine Caron. Permission has been granted to publish the translation of two poems by Pierre Seghers, "J'émerge à peine de l'obscur" and "Je vis comme un trésor caché."

I owe many thanks to my first teachers, Barbara Rockman and Miriam Sagan, for guidance that broadened my vision and helped me move forward.

A particular appreciation goes to my poet friends in France, including Francine Caron, Marie Cayol, Eric Sivry and Nicole Barrière, whose level of commitment and gracious critiques have inspired my writing and translations. I am grateful also to the Société des Intuitistes in Paris for its warm support.

I extend my deep gratitude to the members of the Monday night writing group who saw some of these poems in early drafts, Rachelle Woods, Debbi Brody, Mary-Charlotte Domandi, Ann Hunkins, Mary McGinnis and Elizabeth Raby.

Many thanks to Dorothy Alexander and Poetry Downtown, which is now hosting poets in person. I'm grateful to Jane Shoenfeld and Georgia Jones-Davis for our thoughtful conversations exploring the art of poetry.

I want to extend special gratitude to my mentor, poet Lise Goett, whose intuition and care gave shape to this book.

Many thanks to Joni Arends for her attentive proof-reading.

Basia Miller's poetry has appeared in *The Santa Fe Literary Review, Trickster, Lummox, The Minimum Wager* and other literary journals of note, including French journals such as *Poésie-sur-Seine* and *Portulan bleu*. Her work has been anthologized in collections such as *Malala: Poems for Malala Yousefzai, Mo' Joe, Fixed and Free, The New Mexico Poetry Anthology,* and *Voyage Grand-Tournesol.* Miller co-edited with Alanna C. Burke *Open Spaces*, a selection of haiku from the Santa Fe Haiku Study Group. She was awarded first prize in poetry in the *Santa Fe New Mexican*'s poetry contests in 2018 and 2020. She has published a chapbook, *Carrying Words,* and two books of her poems, with translations by French poets Marie Cayol and Francine Caron, *The Next Village/Le prochain Village* and *Backyard Tree/L'Arbre côté cour.*

Basia Miller recognized her love for poetry after a twenty-year career on the faculty of St. John's College-Santa Fe. She undertook with colleagues Anne Cohler and Harold Stone a scholarly English-language edition of Montesquieu's *Spirit of the Laws* (Cambridge University Press), the first since the eighteenth century. Miller has also translated works by Francine Caron for collectors' editions, including *Cantate pour le Grand Canyon* with original art by Pierre Cayol. Miller currently resides in Santa Fe, New Mexico.

www.ingramcontent.com/pod-product-compliance
Lightning Source LLC
Chambersburg PA
CBHW021203090426
42740CB00008B/1212